A Day in the Life: Rain Forest Animals

Tarantula

Anita Ganeri

Heinemann Library
Chicago, IL

www.heinemannraintree.com
Visit our website to find out more information about Heinemann-Raintree books.

To order:
☎ Phone 888-454-2279
🖥 Visit www.heinemannraintree.com to browse our catalog and order online.

© 2011 Heinemann Library
an imprint of Capstone Global Library, LLC
Chicago, Illinois

Edited by Nancy Dickmann, Rebecca Rissman, and Catherine Veitch
Designed by Steve Mead
Picture research by Mica Brancic
Originated by Capstone Global Library
Printed and bound in China by South China Printing Company Ltd

14 13 12 11 10
10 9 8 7 6 5 4 3 2 1

Library of Congress Cataloging-in-Publication Data
Ganeri, Anita, 1961-
  Tarantula / Anita Ganeri.
    p. cm.—(A day in the life. Rain forest animals)
  Includes bibliographical references and index.
  ISBN 978-1-4329-4109-3 (hc)—ISBN 978-1-4329-4120-8 (pb) 1. Tarantulas—Juvenile literature. I. Title.
  QL458.42.T5G36 2011
  595.4'4—dc22
                                         2010000970

Acknowledgments
We would like to thank the following for permission to reproduce photographs: Ardea pp. 6, 23 fang (Andy Teare); Corbis pp. 7 (© David A. Northcott), 14, 23 silk (© Michael & Patricia Fogden), 20 (© Radius Images); FLPA pp. 9, 17, 23 exoskeleton (Minden Pictures/Mark Moffett), 11 (Minden Pictures/James Christensen); Photolibrary pp. 4 (age fotostock/John Cancalosi), 5 (Oxford Scientific (OSF)/John Mitchell), 12, 15, 23 prey, 23 spiderling (Oxford Scientific (OSF)/Emanuele Biggi), 13, 16 (Oxford Scientific (OSF)/Nick Gordon), 22 (Oxford Scientific (OSF)/Robert Oelman); Photoshot pp. 10, 23 burrow (NHPA), 18 (NHPA/Jany Sauvanet), 19 (NHPA/Daniel Heuclin), 21 (© NHPA/George Bernard); Shutterstock p. 23 rain forest (© Szefei).

Cover photograph of a South American zebra tarantula reproduced with permission of Shutterstock (worldswildlifewonders).

Back cover photographs of (left) a tarantula's burrow reproduced with permission of FLPA (Minden Pictures/Mark Moffett); and (right) a tarantula spiderling reproduced with permission of Photolibrary (Oxford Scientific (OSF)/Emanuele Biggi).

We would like to thank Michael Bright for his invaluable help in the preparation of this book.

Every effort has been made to contact copyright holders of material reproduced in this book. Any omissions will be rectified in subsequent printings if notice is given to the publisher.

Contents

What Is a Tarantula? 4

What Do Tarantulas Look Like? 6

Where Do Tarantulas Live? 8

What Do Tarantulas Do at Night? 10

What Do Tarantulas Eat? 12

Where Are Baby Tarantulas Born? 14

How Do Tarantulas Grow? 16

What Do Tarantulas Do During the Day? 18

What Hunts Tarantulas? 20

Tarantula Body Map 22

Glossary 23

Find Out More 24

Index 24

Some words are in bold, **like this**. You can find them in the glossary on page 23.

What Is a Tarantula?

Tarantulas are very big spiders.

All spiders have eight legs and their bodies are divided into two parts.

Goliath birdeater

There are many different types of tarantulas.

The largest kind of tarantula is known as the Goliath birdeater.

What Do Tarantulas Look Like?

fang

Tarantulas have large, round bodies.

They have strong jaws and poisonous **fangs**.

eyes

A tarantula has a group of tiny eyes on top of its head.

Its body and legs are covered in tiny hairs.

Where Do Tarantulas Live?

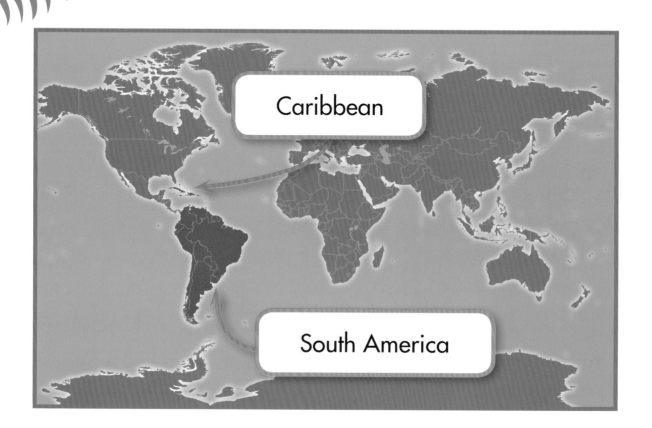

Caribbean

South America

Many tarantulas live in the **rain forests** of South America and the Caribbean.

It is warm and wet in the rain forests.

burrow

Some tarantulas live on the rain forest floor under rocks or logs.

Others dig **burrows** in the ground.

What Do Tarantulas Do at Night?

At night, a tarantula may leave its **burrow** to look for food.

It crawls slowly across the forest floor, but it does not travel very far.

Then the tarantula waits for its **prey** to come close.

It grabs its prey and kills it with a bite from its poisonous **fangs**.

What Do Tarantulas Eat?

frog

Tarantulas mainly eat **rain forest** insects and other spiders.

They can also catch frogs, snakes, small lizards, and small birds.

After a meal, a tarantula does not need to eat again for a whole month.

It sits in its **burrow** until it needs to go hunting again.

Where Are Baby Tarantulas Born?

eggs inside a silk bag

Baby tarantulas are born in a **burrow** at night.

The female lays hundreds of eggs and wraps them in a **silk** bag.

spiderling

The female guards the eggs until the **spiderlings** hatch.

The spiderlings leave the burrow when they are about two weeks old.

How Do Tarantulas Grow?

exoskeleton

A tarantula has a hard skin around its body called an **exoskeleton**.

As the tarantula grows bigger, its skin becomes too tight.

old skin

The tarantula pushes itself out of its old skin.

It has new, bigger skin underneath.

What Do Tarantulas Do During the Day?

burrow

During the day, a tarantula rests in its **burrow**.

It does not sleep the same way you do.

hairs

If the tarantula is disturbed, it gives a loud hiss.

Then it flicks hairs from its body into its attacker's face.

What Hunts Tarantulas?

grilled tarantulas

Rain forest animals such as lizards, snakes, and birds hunt tarantulas to eat.

People also eat tarantulas.

hawk wasp

Hawk wasps hunt tarantulas while they rest during the day.

A wasp stings a spider to stop it from moving. It uses the spider as food for its young.

Tarantula Body Map

hairs

leg

eye

mouthpart

Glossary

 **burrow** hole in the ground that animals live in

 **exoskeleton** hard skin around a spider's body

 **fang** sharp body part like a tooth. It squeezes out poison.

 **prey** animal that is hunted by other animals for food

 **rain forest** thick forest with very tall trees and a lot of rain

 **silk** soft, strong material made by spiders

 **spiderling** baby spider

Find Out More

Books

Bredeson, Carmen. *Hair-Shooting Tarantulas and Other Weird Spiders.* Berkeley Heights, NJ: Enslow, 2010.

Twist, Clink. *Tarantulas.* Milwaukee, WI: Gareth Stevens, 2006.

Websites

http://animals.nationalgeographic.com/animals/bugs/tarantula.html

http://a-z-animals.com/animals/red-knee-tarantula/

www.itsnature.org/ground/creepy-crawlies-land/red-kneed-tarantula

Index

babies 14, 15
burrow 9, 10, 13, 14, 15, 18
Caribbean 8
defence 19
eggs 14, 15
eyes 7, 22

exoskeleton 16
fangs 6, 11
feeding 10, 11, 12, 13
hawk wasps 21
South America 8
spiderlings 15